I0786395

EXAMINATION OF THE CHILDHOOD SEXUAL ABUSE AMONG NIGERIAN WOMEN LIVING IN THE STATE OF GEORGIA AND ALABAMA, AND THEIR COPING STRATEGIES.

Florence Agbasi-Moemena, Ed.D

Licensed Professional Counselor, U.S.A.

Adjunct Professor, U.S.A.

June 1, 2018

ABSTRACT

This study was carried out to examine the childhood sexual abuse among Nigerian women living in the State of Georgia and Alabama and their coping strategies.

Aim*: The purpose of this study is to uncover the childhood sexual abuse of Nigerian women and bring to awareness, the impact and need for support or treatment.*

Background*: Child sexual abuse in Nigeria is increasing at an alarming rate and not much is being done to help the victim or educate the public.*

Method*: A validated questionnaire was used for the face to face interview of 246 randomly selected Nigeria women of different ethnic groups.*

Result*: The outcome of this research shows that Nigerians face childhood sexual abuse from the tender age of 3 to 17 years and that Nigerians are less likely to use counseling in solving problems even when proven to be beneficial.*

Conclusion*: Childhood sexual abuse are rarely reported in Nigeria because of the victims' fear of repercussion. To help curb this crime in Nigeria, existing laws should be enforced, and lapses reviewed while complaints of sex crime properly handled.*

Keyword: Childhood sexual abuse, Neglect, exploitation, coping strategies, counseling, self-help,

Introduction

The existence of child sexual abuse in Nigeria cannot be denied. This has been reported in various forms, the media and researches. The case of child sexual abuse is a problem yet to be solved or eradicated. In order to handle this problem as it affects the victims and that of the culprits, there has been suggestions by individuals, researchers, and even laws passed by government on this issue.

In spite of many researchers' effort to come up with unvarying definition of child sexual abuse, there are still discrepancies in the way each individual researcher defines childhood sexual abuse.

Statement of the problem

Childhood sexual abuse is considered a criminal act nearly everywhere in the world and is usually treated with strict criminal penalties including life imprisonment or capital punishment in some jurisdictions (Levesque, 1999). In many Nigerian public schools, there are high occurrences of sex abuse (Owuananam 1995). Similarly, Uwajare (2013) indicated that a 37-year-old man was arrested for raping his 17-year-old daughter whom he has impregnated three times. Based on these facts cited, it is clear that childhood sexual abuse also exists in Nigeria. Thus, the crux of this study is to uncover the childhood sexual abuse of Nigerian women living in the state of Georgia and Alabama and how they have dealt with the abuse.

Definition of Sexual Abuse

Child sexual abuse, according to Finkehor, (1984) is sexual contact with a minor that occurs as a result of force or in a relationship where an adult sexually exploits a child. Finkelhor, Hotaling, Lewis, and Smith (1990) also noted that the definition of sexual abuse of children vary depending on the disciplines, social system, research efforts, and laws. They mentioned that there are many forms of child sexual abuse, and they include but are not limited to rape, fondling, sexual assault, exposure, voyeurism, and the commercial sexual exploitation of children. The impact of childhood sexual abuse can lead to long term psychological effect depending on the severity of the abuse. Some of the victims experience posttraumatic stress disorder, depression, anxiety or indulge in drug or alcohol abuse. There is also self-blaming, engaging in dissociative behavior, eating problem, experiencing shame, experiencing relationship difficulty, and sexual problems (Hall and Hall 2011).

The various research reports cited above confirm the existence of child sexual abuse, but there is no resolution for these problems.

Issues of Childhood Sexual Abuse

Adults, especially women, who were abused during childhood, are more likely to be at risk of re-victimization later in life (Widom, Czaja, & Dutton, 2008). According to Miller-Perrin & Perrin, (2007) however, the effect of child abuse and neglect that spread into adulthood will differ significantly. While for some adults the effect may be chronic and debilitating, for some, the outcome may be positive, despite the above. Miller-Perrin and Perrin (2007) also listed some of the factors that may have impact on the way child abuse affects adults as follows: age of occurrence and severity, frequency and duration of the abuse, relationship of the abuser with the perpetrator, type of abuse, action taken to ensure the safety of the child when abuse was detected, and whether the victim or the survivor received the appropriate treatment, such as therapy and support. Brown & Finkelho, (1986) indicated that survivors of childhood sexual abuse tend to display more self-destructive behaviors and experience suicidal ideation than those who have not been abused. Ratican (1992) concluded that child sexual abuse leads to difficulty trusting others, establishing interpersonal boundaries or engaging in intimate relationships, and getting involved in abusive relationships.

McQueen, Itzin, Kennedy, Sinason, and Maxted (2009) noted that the effects of child abuse and neglect are still largely hidden and may emerge at key times later in life indicating that:

> abusive experiences in adulthood can resurrect old wounds of past child abuse or neglect that may lead to further adverse effects for the survivors Pg. 67.

The views of McQueen et al has left a need to find curative solutions for this plague called childhood sexual abuse.

The Nature of Sexual Abuse in Nigeria

The area of child sexual abuse within Nigeria is under researched, and this is largely due to the fact that discussions on the abuse is still seen as a taboo and something to be dealt with privately. Many studies point to the epidemic of sexual abuse of Nigerian children and Nigerian's reluctance to seek prevention or help. Studies also show that many of the victims in Nigeria experience difficulty disclosing the abuse due to fear of repercussion such as bringing shame to the family, fear of what the perpetrator may do, fear of the accusation of lying about the abuse, and if the perpetrator is the breadwinner, fear of jeopardizing things for the family financially after the breadwinner's imprisonment.

In Bosede (2012), on the discussion of the 1999 African Network for the Prevention and Protection against Child Abuse and Neglect (ANPPCA), the study regarding 100 female Ibadan metropolis hawkers and 100 non-Ibadan metropolis female hawkers between 8-15 years old revealed that out of the 200 female hawkers, 50% of them were coerced into sexual intercourse, 9% of the hawkers were forced to sexual intercourse during errands or when walking to or from school. Only 7% of these girls reported the incident to their parents or guardians. The reason was cited to be because of fear of stigma or ridicule if the abuse is made public. The Nigerian 1999 Demographic Health Survey (NDHS) also shows that over 25% of adolescent in Nigeria have had their first sexual intercourse by age 15 and many through rape. The challenging factor stems from Nigeria lacking the precise prevention information and the required crisis intervention and response. Sexual abuse has been classified by some Nigerian researchers as a public health epidemic that lacks medical treatment.

Ikechubelu, Udegwe, Ezechukwu, Ndinechi, (2008) concluded in their research regarding sexual abuse of female hawkers in Anambra State, Nigeria, that

> Out of 186 respondents, 69% had been sexually abused with 17% having had penetrative sexual intercourse (28% were forced) and 56% submitted willingly while hawking. The mean age of the female hawkers was listed as 13.0 +/ - 2.2 years. Pg. 114- 116.

Another study conducted by University Teaching Hospital (Obstetrics, Gynecology & Pathology Department) Jos, Nigeria on rape, revealed that 63% of the victims were children within the infantile age group. The study concluded that 26.7% accounted for girls under 16 years of age are at an increased risk of being sexually coerced or raped, possibly because they are defenseless and vulnerable and also that children and young adolescents are more at risk than adults to be raped (Daru, Mutihir, Silas & Ekwempu, 2011).

The various forms of sexual abuse in Nigeria, according to Fawole, Ajuwon, Osungbade, and Fawaye, (2002); Obisesan, Adeyemo, and Onifade, (1999); Olufemi-Kayode, (2004) varies from 2% to 56%, while Ige and Fawole in their 2011 research on child sexual abuse (CSA) showed 84% of the respondents agreeing that CSA occurred in their community, but only 34% agreed that it could have serious health impact. Furthermore, 46.8% of the parents felt their children could not become victims of CSA (Fawole & Ige 2011). Elementary students and adolescent girls between ages 13-19 were noted by Olusanya, Ogbemi, Unuigbe, and Oronsaye (1986) as the major victims of rape.

Nigerian widely read Newspaper, the Sun, in its December 29, 2013 issue, reported the arrest of a 37-year-old man for raping his 17-year-old daughter and impregnating her three times. The incident came out when his daughter became pregnant the third time and was unwilling to go for an abortion again; instead, she alerted the neighbors (Uwajare, 2013). Another report also showed a father in Abuja area who impregnated his daughter, rejected the child, and decided, however, that traditional rituals be performed to ward off what is regarded as "evil repercussions of the abominable act" (Thomas, 2010).

The average age of marriage in Kebbi State of Northern Nigeria is 11 years old, and half of the girls within this area of Nigeria marry by the time they reach 16 years old (Krug, Dahlberg, Mercy, Zwi & Lozano (2002). These men that indulge in the exploitation and rape of children are cognizant of what they are doing but justify their actions by pledging to not have sex with the children until they reach puberty, which is an empty promise considering the high rate of rape and child sex slavery within Northern Nigeria. This explains why a 49-year-old man who is a state representative (Nigerian Senator) married a 13-year-old Egyptian girl and even voted to allow for Nigeria to pass a law whereby married girls will be considered women (Hirsch, 2013). It is inconceivable that a senator who obviously is a pedophile is placed in position to uphold the law to stop pedophiles; rather, he is putting children in harm's way.

These children in the northern part of Nigeria that are being ushered off for marriage and then raped suffer multiple health risks, and the most rampant is Vesico-Vaginal Fistula (VVF), whereby damage to the pelvis causes urine to drip continuously from the bladder into the vagina. In addition, these girls are often ostracized by others due to their condition. Many of the women affected by VVF are mainly from remote villages of the northern states of Nigeria. These northern states lack healthcare facilities, and the girls are extremely poor with high percentage of illiteracy Sanusi (2013). The current Emir of Kano and former Nigerian Central Bank indicated that as many as 93% of female children in the northern region of Nigeria are denied access to secondary education while 70% of the women between 20 and 29 years of age are unable to read in comparison to 9.7 percent of their counterparts in the south-west.

Nigeria Law on Sex Crime

Nigeria has a law regarding sex crime, which is identified in section 357 of their Criminal Code Act, CAP 77, LFN 1990, and defines rape as follows:

> Any person who has unlawful carnal knowledge of a woman or girl, without her consent, or with her consent, if the consent is obtained by force or by means of false threats or intimidation of any kind, or by fear of harm, or by means of false or fraudulent representation as to the nature of the act, or in case of a married woman, by personating her husband is guilty of an offence called rape Sex. 357.

The disturbing factor about this law of federation of Nigeria (LFN, 1990) is that it is decades old and needs to be amended. There is nothing in the law that addresses when a man is raped, and studies show continuous and unresolved sexual crimes within Nigeria. The law should be amended to include boys while also reinforcing the laws already put in place for girls.

Nigerian Penal Code explains that rape is a criminal offence that is punishable by imprisonment of up to 14 years, which can be combined with a fine and up to 7 years in the case of child-related sexual assault (defilement). The criminal Code in Section 358 also provides that rape is punishable by "life imprisonment," with the possibility of additional punishment. There is not much evidence indicating that sufficient and persistent punishment is occurring when this crime happens in order to deter the criminals, but in many instances, affordable bail is granted even in the case of child rape, thereby, compounding the problem rather than ensuring proper justice.

Dedeigbo and Akunoka (2013) of Lagos PM daily Newspaper reported an incident where a 34-year-old man raped a 3-year-old and was granted a bail on a N250,000 (About $700). This amount does not commensurate to corrective measures that need to be put in place by the Nigerian government for the damage that is done to the child.

International Law on Child Sexual Abuse

In United States and a few other countries, when an adult rape a child or engages in sexual intercourse with a child below the legal age of consent, it is considered statutory rape. This is based on the standard that a child is not capable of consenting; therefore, any perceptible consent by a child is not considered to be legal. If Nigeria starts to fully enforce this standard, it will help deter sex offenders. Oftentimes, perpetrators blame the victims when caught, claiming the child agreed to it, especially when the child is coerced.

Often times, female students in Nigerian schools are lured by male teachers into having sex. Owuamanam (1995) noted what prevents the female students from refusing the sexual advances of the teachers include "physical, psychological or social consequences." As Owuamanam explained, the relationship between female students and their teachers involve power and struggles. Since the teachers have power over the students in Nigeria, that limits the students' ability to refuse the sexual advances due to fear of retaliation from the teachers. A "no" to sexual advances by a teacher in a Nigerian public institution may affect the student's grades regardless of her academic ability or performance. Nigerian law does very little to protect students of this crime. It is essential to help educate the masses about the problem as this author sees as worthy of research and prevention.

Methodology

This study was done utilizing face to face survey design. The population was made up of 300 Nigerian women living in the state of Georgia and Alabama. The distribution of the population is shown in table 1.

Table 1: **Population of the Study (20-65years)**

City	Tribe			
	Ibo	**Calabr**	**Yoruba**	**Total**
Columbus Georgia	60	20	10	90
Atlanta Georgia	50	5	40	95
Phenix City Alabama	40	10	5	55
Montgomery Alabama	40	5	15	60
	190	**40**	**70**	**300**

Instrument used for the Study

A check list questionnaire was designed for the face to face interview. The interview question sought information on childhood sexual abuse of the women.

Data Analysis

The percentage analysis formula was used to analyze data collected and a score of 50% and above was accepted as a positive. 246 (82%) out of the 300 respondents were successfully interviewed. The analysis is presented in tables.

Research Question 1

Has there been childhood sexual abuse on Nigeria women living in the states of Georgia and Alabama?

Table 2

Nigeria women response on childhood sexual abuse.

N = 246

S/N	Item		Frequency	Percentage
1a	Are you a Nigeria?	Yes	246	100
		No	–	–
1b	If yes indicate your ethic group			
	i. Ibo		136	55
	ii. Calabar		40	16
	iii. Ija		--	--
	iv. Yoruba		70	28
	v. Hausa		--	--
2a	Please state your marital status			
	i. Single		56	23
	ii. Married		150	61
	iii. Divorced		40	16
Table 2 continued				
2b	Please say your status			
	i. Student		40	16
	ii. Unemployed		35	14
	iii. Self employed		35	14
	iv. Professionals:- Health care, lawyer		66	26
	v. Homemaker/housekeeper		40	16
	vi. Clerks		30	12
3a	Have you experienced sexual abuse	Yes	246	100
		No	–	–
3b	If yes say how it happened			
	i. You were sexually touched (oral, anal, virginal sex) during your childhood.		158	64
	ii. You were forced top have sex during your childhood.		220	89
	iii. You were involved in unwanted sex during your childhood.		160	66
	If you have experienced sexual abuse state who did it			
4	i. Your father			
	ii. Your brother		156	63
	iii. Your cousin/nephew/uncle		150	61
	iv. A family friend		200	81
	v. A distant relation/in-law		103	
	vi. Your school teacher		180	73
	vii. A fellow student		160	66
	A member of your peer group		30	12
	viii. An unknown person		40	16
	ix. A neighbor		76	
	x. A barbar		160	66
	xi. A primary physician		80	33
	xii. A clergy		90	37
	xiii. A church official		156	63

5	At what age did you experience sexual abuse?	140	57
	i. 3-7 years	200	81
	ii. 8-12 years	190	77
	iii. 13-17 years	210	85
	iv. 18 – 22 years	30	12
	v. 22 and above	20	8

Research Question 2

How did the Nigeria women cope with the childhood sexual abuse?

Table 3

Nigeria women response on how they dealt with childhood sexual abuse

N = 246

S/N	Item		Frequency	Percentage
6a	Did you take any action when you experience sexual abuse?			
		Yes	80	33
		No	166	67
6b	If yes state the action you took			
	i. You reported to your parents/guardian		27	34
	ii. You reported the incident to a friend		31	39
	iii. You reported the incident to your siblings		20	25
	iv. You reported the incident to a trusted adult		2	3
6c	If No state your reasons			
	i. Because of fear of being punished/Not believed		143	86
	ii. Fear of being labeled a trouble maker by the perpetrators, family, friends or other family members.		94	57
	iii. Other (Specify)		–	–
7a	Where you provided with help or any form of treatment when the sexual abuse occurred?	Yes	102	41
		No	144	59
7b	If yes say the action taken at that time			
	i. Taken to a traditional healer ("Juju man") to cleanse the taboo		73	72
	ii. "undoing" what was done by traditional healer		73	72
	iii. Taken to therapy		–	–
	iv. Clergy		21	20
	v. Other/Medical treatment		6	6
7c	Was the treatment provided to you helpful?			
		Yes	31	30
		No	71	69
7d	If no say the reasons			
	i. It resulted in further sexual exploitation and rape		62	87
	ii. No appropriate help was received		62	87
	iii. Experiencing instability and difficulty in relationship		49	69
	iv. Lack of trust		69	97
	v. Other reasons (Specify)		–	–
8a	Did you seek help when you became older?			
		Yes	137	56
		No	109	43
8b	If Yes state how			
	i. Talked to trusted individuals when you became older		35	26

Table 3 continued

	ii. Talked with the clergy and through prayers	52	41
	iii. Sought Counseling	19	13
	iv. Started creating self-awareness through reading	22	16
	v. Educating other women when the opportunity occurs	12	9
	vi. Involvement with volunteer but did not disclose the abuse	15	11
	vii. Other (Specify)	—	-
8c	Were the steps you took useful and beneficial?		
	Yes	104	76
	No	33	24
8d	If Yes how?		
	i. These steps helped to stabilize me towards living a meaningful life	81	78
	ii. It helped to relax your mind towards the trauma of sexual abuse	64	62
	iii. If helped to stabilize your life activities in relation to the trauma	60	58
	iv. It helped achieve success in your endeavors	89	86
	v. Other (Specify)	-	-
8e	Specify the steps that were useful to you		
	i. Talked to trusted individuals when you became older	18	51
	ii. Talked with the clergy and through prayers	31	60
	iii. Sought Counseling	17	89
	iv. Started creating self-awareness through reading	11	50
	v. Educating other women when the opportunity arise/	7	32
	vi. Involvement with voluntary activities but did not disclose the abuse	9	60
9e	Where you aware of using professional counseling in solving problems or dealing with the abuse as you became older		
	Yes	246	100
	No	42	17
10	If you did not seek counseling in dealing with the trauma, state your reasons		
	i Inability to pay for it	19	8
	ii Not sure where or how to seek for it	200	81
	iii Fear of stigmatization	-	-
	iv other	-	-

DISCUSSION ON THE FINDINGS

The findings of this study revealed that there has been childhood sexual abuse of Nigerian women living in the states of Georgia and Alabama, and many of the victims did not seek professional treatment or support. Out of the 246 respondents, 50 are single, 150 married, and 40 are divorcees. The occupational status of the respondents includes students, unemployed, self-employed, health care professionals, lawyers, home makers, housekeepers and clerks.

158 (64%) out of the 246 women indicated they were sexually abused orally, through anal and virginal; 220 (89%) said they were forced, and 160 (66%) were involved in unwanted sex.

The age range of the sexual abuse occurrences reported by the respondents is 3 to 17 years old as shown in table 2.

67% of the respondents never took any action when they experienced sexual abuse. 86% of the respondents did not report the incidents because of fear of being punished, while 57% of the respondents' fear being labeled a trouble maker by the perpetrator's family, friends or from taking any action.

 33% of the respondents reported the case, while 67% did not report the case. 72% of the respondents who reported the case were taken to what is known as in Igbo language "Dibia" i.e. traditional healer ("Juju man") to cleanse the taboo and undo what was done, but 59% of the respondents said that they were not given any treatment. 69% of the respondents said that the traditional method was not helpful. Their response positively revealed that traditional treatment rather resulted in further sexual exploitation, rape, instability, difficulty in relationship, including non-receipt of appropriate help and lack of trust. This type of action shows that Nigerians are detached when it comes to sexual abuse even when it is shown that the nonchalant approach is not helpful.

The result also revealed that few of the women that sought counseling, engaged in creating self-awareness, educating other women, talking to the clergy, or engaging in voluntary activities. Some found these things to be helpful in overcoming the abuse, while some never disclosed the abuse.

CONCLUSION

Based on the findings, the following conclusions have been drawn. Nigerian women face childhood sexual abuse from the tender age of 3 to 17 years old. As a result of the nonchalant attitude of the Nigerian law enforcement agencies and parents of child sexual abuse victims, sex crimes in Nigeria on minors are increasing. The perpetrators range from fathers, brothers, and uncles to religious and unknown persons. The abuse is rarely reported or exposed because of the victim's fear of being punished or labeled a trouble maker by the perpetrators.

In some cases, after the abuse is reported, relatives take the victims to traditional healers (Juju man) as shown in table 3. This approach is not helpful in coping with the abuse; rather, it results in further exploitation or rape of the victims by the very people that supposed to help.

RECOMMENDATION

Based on the findings of this study, the following recommendations are made:

The existing laws in Nigeria should be enforced regarding sexual crime and any lapse(s) within the law should also be reviewed and amended where necessary.

Functional programs that will help to educate children or survivors of sexual abuse on their rights towards the control of their body should be established in Nigeria

Children should be properly educated on different parts of their body

Children should be encouraged to alert adults when someone touches them inappropriately.

Nigerian government should establish fully function centers for people to report sex crimes to enable crime agents to pursue such case.

Nigerian Law Enforcement Officers, particularly police officers, should be involved in ensuring the safety of children and prevention of abuse. This can be done through proper training of the police and allocation of resources towards problem of sexual abuse.

Furthermore, fully functioning culture sensitive prevention program that will target the parents and educate them about sexual abuse should be put in place because when parents are educated, they can, in turn, educate their children. This will help the parents become aware of potential abusers and identify warning signs of sexual abuse they may be overlooking. It will also help parents become aware of the impact of child sexual abuse and the fact that going to the traditional healer cannot "undo" what happened or result in cleansing the abuse.

Complaints of sex crime should be properly handled and necessary paper work safe guarded. Any police or law enforcement that accepts bribe instead of working towards solving the problem should be dealt with severely.

Further studies are recommended that will include all Nigerian ethnic groups to help in seeing whether the number of years spent in the United States by Nigerians will affect their willingness to seek professional counseling for sexual abuse or other emotional issues.

One of the goals of this researcher is to help bring awareness, the need for counseling and support for Nigerians experiencing psychological or emotional difficulties. It is therefore recommended that Mental Health Professionals who are interested in working with Nigerians or combating mental illness among Nigerians, become familiar with Nigeria culture and their philosophical approach in handling problems.

Continued education in multicultural counseling specifically regarding how to work with Nigerians in general is also recommended to help increase Nigerians interest in professional counseling.

References

Bosede, A.F (2012). Child sexual abuse: A potential damage to children, Ado-Ekiti, Nigeria. *Journal of Educational and Social Research vol.2 (2).*

Browne, A., & Finkelhor, D. (1986), Impact of child sexual abuse: Psychological Bulletin, Vol. 99, No. 1, 66-77. *American Psychological Association, USA; University of New Hampshire.*

Carlin, A.S. & Ward, N.C. (1992). Subtypes of psychiatric inpatient women who have been sexually abused in *J Nerv Dis. 1992 June; 180(6): 392-7. PubMed PMID: 1593274*

Daru, E.O, Osagie, I.C., Pam, JT, Mutihir, OA, Ekwempu, CC (2011). Analysis of cases of rape as seen at the Jos University Teaching Hospital, Jos, north central Nigeria. *Nigerian Journal of Clinical Practice Vol. 14 Issue 1.*

Dedeigbo, A, & Okunola, D (2013). Man, 34, Charged with Raping 3-Yr Old. (PICTURED). Daily P.M. Newspaper Lagos, Nigeria. *PM Publishing Ltd, February 25.*

Fawole, I. O. Ajuwon, A., Osungbade, K., & Faweya, O. (2002). Prevalence and nature of violence among young female hawkers in motor-parks in south-western. Nigeria. *Health Education, 102, 230–238. Research Paper. Bingley; Emerald Group Publishing Limited.*

Fawole, I. O. & Ige O. K. (2011) Preventing Child Sexual Abuse: Parents' Perceptions and Practices in Urban Nigeria. *Journal of Child Sexual Abuse, 20:695–707. University College hospital Ibadan Nigeria. Published online.*

Finkelhor, D. (1984) Child Sexual Abuse: New Theory and Research. New York. USA; Free Press Publishing.

Finkelhor, D., Hotaling, G., Lewis, I.A., & Smith, C. (1990). Sexual abuse in a national survey of adult men and women: *Prevalence, characteristics, and risk factors. Child Abuse and Neglect, 14(1), p. 19-28. USA: University of New Hampshire Associates Inc.*

Hall, M., & Hall, J. (2011). The long-term effects of childhood sexual abuse: Counseling implications. Retrieved August 29, 2013 from *http://counselingoutfitters.com/vistas/vistas11/Article_19.pdf*

Hirsch, A, (2013). Nigerian senator who 'married girl of 13' accused of breaking Child Rights Act. Lagos: The Guardian, Guardian, Newspaper Ltd. July 25 issue.

Idowu, A (1985). Counseling Nigerian Students in United States colleges and universities. *Journal of Counseling and Psychology vol. 63 500-509. New Jersey; Wiley Blackwell Hoboken.*

Ikechebelu, J. I, Udigwe, G O; Ezechukwu, C C, Ndinechi, A G; Joe-Ikechebelu (2008). Sexual abuse among juvenile female street hawkers in Anambra State, Nigeria. Ugbowo, Benin City; *African Journal of Reproductive Health Nigeria 12 (2) 111-119.*

Krug E.G, Dahlberg, L., Mercy, J.A. Zwi, A.B, & Lozano, R. (2002). World Report on violence and health. World Health Organization, Geneva, Switzerland. Retrieved from http://www.who.int/violence_injury_prevention/violence/world_report/en/summary_en.pdf Aprl 18, 2014.

Levesque R. J. (1999). Sexual abuse of Children: A human rights perspective. *Bloomington; Indiana University Press.*

McQueen, D., Itzin, C., Kennedy, R., Sinason, V., & Maxted, F. (2009). *Psychoanalytic psychotherapy after child abuse, London; Karnac Books Ltd.*

Miller-Perrin, C., & Perrin, R. (2007). Child maltreatment: an introduction. USA; Thousand Oaks: Sage Publications.

Obisesan, K. A., Adeyemo, A. A., & Onifade, R. A. (1999). Childhood sexuality and child sexual abuse in southwest Nigeria. *Journal of Obstetrics and Gynecology, 19, 624–626. Ibadan, Nigeria; Informa Healthcare.*

Olufemi-Kayode, P. (2004). Child sexual abuse and HIV/AIDS. Paper presented at the *XV International Conference on AIDS, Bangkok, Thailand.*

Olusanyan O. Ogbemi S., Unigbe J. and Orosaye A. (1986). The pattern of rape in Benin.City. Nigeria. Netherlands; *Journal of Tropical and Geographical Medicine V 38 (3), 215-220. Mediline TA.*

Owuananam D.O. (1995). Youth: The age of contrast in Human development, Ado-Ekiti; the fourth inaugural lecture of Ondo State University, September 22, 1995.

Ratican, K. (1992). Sexual abuse survivors: Identifying symptoms and special treatment considerations. *Journal of Counseling & Development, 71(1), 33-38. U.S.A; American Counseling Association.*

Sanusi. L. (2013). 93% of girls are illiterate in Northern Nigeria. Retrieved from http:www.nigerianwatch.com/news/1585 October 9.

Sijuwola, O. A. (1995). Cultural, religion and mental illness in Nigeria. In 1. *AIISSA (ed), handbook of culture and mental illness (pp65-67). Madison WI: International University Press.*

Swaby, A. N. and Morgan, K. A (2009). The relationship between childhood sexual abuse and sexual dysfunction in Jamaican adults. *Journal of Child Sexual Abuse 18 (3),247-266. USA; Focal Press. Waltham, Massachusetts USA.*

Uwajare N. (2013). Man impregnates daughter three times. Sunday Sun, Sun Newspaper, Lagos; *The Sun Publishing Ltd. December, 29.*

Thomas, T. (2010). Latest on evil dad who fathered daughter's child. Sunday Sun, Sun Newspaper, Lagos; *The Sun Publishing Ltd. November 28.*

Widom, C., Czaja, S., & Dutton, M. (2008). Childhood victimization and lifetime revictimization. *Child abuse and neglect, 32, 785-796 USA; Elsevier Ltd USA.*